Urban Bird Life

Urban Bird Life

Iris Lee

The New York Quarterly Foundation, Inc.
New York, New York

NYQ Books™ is an imprint of The New York Quarterly Foundation, Inc.

The New York Quarterly Foundation, Inc.
P. O. Box 2015
Old Chelsea Station
New York, NY 10113

www.nyqbooks.org

Copyright © 2010 by Iris Lee

All rights reserved. No part of this book may be used or reproduced in any manner whatsoever without written permission of the author. This book is a work of fiction. Any references to historical events, real people or real locales are used fictitiously. Other names, characters, places, and incidents are products of the author's imagination, and any resemblance to actual events or locales or persons, living or dead, is entirely coincidental.

The following poems first appeared elsewhere: "Teresa on the Subway" in *The Subway Chronicles* (as "Morning—Going Uptown"); "Visiting My Coney Island Home," "Beginnings," (as "You Have Been Here"), "Urban Bird Life," "Inspiration," A Sort of Epithalamion," and "Brooklyn Heights, September 12, 2001" in *The New York Quarterly*.

Much appreciation goes to Raymond Hammond, Maxine Rosen and Norman Taffel, and gratitude always to William Packard.

First Edition

Set in New Baskerville

Layout and Design by Raymond P. Hammond

Cover art: *Yellow Field*, 16½ x 20½ inches, gouache, chalk, and collage on paper by Bruce Rosen, ©1993 The Estate of Bruce Rosen | www.brucerosen.com

Author photo by Richard Moses.

Library of Congress Control Number: 2009937603

ISBN: 978-1-935520-16-0

Urban Bird Life

For Laurin and for Philip

Contents

One

City Hall Subway Station	17
Transiting	
Terpsichore in the Subway Station	18
Teresa on the Subway	19
Morning Rush Hour Bridge	20
Evening Bridge	21
Millennium Evening Bridge	22
Lady	23
What Are You Doing Here?	24
Gloves	25
Convenience	26
Building Sites—Sunday	27
Stories	28
Water World	29
Visiting My Coney Island Home	30
Fall Madness	32
Hypothetical Dream of a Former Lover	33
Remembrance of Things	34

Two

Erotica	37
As a Woman Might	38
Late Sex	39
Beginnings	40
Brownstone	42
Sunday Morning, Early Summer	43
A Sort of Epithalamion	44
Very Early One Morning	45
Urban Bird Life	46
Brooklyn Heights, September 12, 2001	47
Moment of Silence: The Second Year	48
How to Lower Your Anxiety After 9/11	49
In the Sicily-Rome American Cemetery November 2001	50
Patriot Rant	51
If You Knew Then…	52

Three

West Fourth Street Station	57
Two for William Packard	
Elegy for Bill	58
Where I Am When I Find Out	59
My Dead Mother Comes to My Imaginary Poetry Reading	60
The Drinking Lives	63
Dead Artist Opening	64
Haunted	65
Antony Abandons Dionysus	66
Shylock, After	68
Edward Hopper in Nyack	69
Bartleby at Rest	70
Ralph Eugene Meatyard Photography Exhibit	71
My Next Duchess	72
Last of the Duke	73
En Attendant Beckett	74

Four

"That time of year thou mayst in me behold..."	77
Rain	78
Cadman Plaza Park at 8am	79
Chilly for May	80
Believe	81
Green Survivor	82
Walking with Laurin	83
Low Tide	84
Night Storm at the Beach	85
Atlantic 6:45 a.m.	86
Something Like Peace	87
Ars Poetica	88
Birth Cries	89
Tempus Fugit	90
Untethered	91
Accumulations	92
Playground Science	93
What You Learn in the Dark	94
Not Swan Lake	95
What Stirs	96
Inspiration	97
Implausible	98

All things must change, to something new, to something strange.

Henry Wadsworth Longfellow

One

CITY HALL SUBWAY STATION

Rising from the curving tunnel
the uptown "N" train bathes
the white tile wall in yellow light.
A sparrow lands on the platform.

The light,
the bird.

The train will move on to Canal
once I step in.
Yet for the moment my dead mother
floats through this station, summoned by

the light,
the bird.

It's many years ago. You're thin.
You steer me to a seat.
You hold me on your lap
to free a seat for someone else's

mother.
Mother,

Will you be here again tomorrow morning?
We could ride these roaring tunnels,
you could teach me not to be afraid,
we'd run away from home,

birds
in light.

TRANSITING

1. TERPSICHORE IN THE SUBWAY SYSTEM

Plastic bags,
natural dancers,
navigate obstacles,
partner each other, glide
on underground currents
up and down station stairs.

2. TERESA ON THE SUBWAY

It's too warm
on the #4 train
Teresa
stuffs her purple parka
behind her
Her mother's busy with
the baby
Teresa twirls her hair-
band in her
right hand   With each 4 or
5 twirls it
falls on the subway floor
She scoops it
up, slides her eyes toward her
mother and
snuggles up against her
one free arm.

3. MORNING RUSH HOUR BRIDGE

Cars crowd the Bridge.
No stars, no moon, no planets linger.
The occasional helicopter
grumbles its way up the river.
Its twinkle turns into a raucous beam,
intruding on our high-rise lives.

4. EVENING BRIDGE

The party boat
glides under the Bridge
and oh what a night
to be on the River
as day ends and lights
from scows and tugs
relieve the fog's gray foam.
Now a skyscraper
takes shape across the River.
Tiny lights
left by the night crew
will burn through to morning.

5. MILLENNIUM EVENING BRIDGE

Begun with fog
and blurred yellow lights
in the park across the street,
the awaited day ended with a bloody sun
behind a scrim of cloud.
The haze remained
as I held vigil at the open window
watching couples
cross the Brooklyn Bridge
even as the temperature began to fall.
Everyone on the radio said
everything worked out.

LADY

her coat
the bus is
late
frayed
late
frayed
cuffs
she'll be
late for work
cocoa brown
late fall
shawl collar
count change
weather change
rabbit fur
far down the street
the bus is
she is
changed
charged late
collar is frayed
for work
is not warm
is worn
the bus is
warned
late.

WHAT ARE YOU DOING HERE?

Two Indian men
carefully folding a white tarp
on a brownstone stoop
Monday morning in Brooklyn Heights
do contract work,
renovating homes for owners
who want them to finish
before the children return with their nannies.
Children shouldn't need to navigate
that debris-strewn stoop.

Indian men don't care
for blonde children, Jamaican nannies
staring at their turbans,
so they stow tarps in truck,
leaving steps carefully swept.

GLOVES

One winter day I logged lost gloves,
the ones I found in: subways, shops, wide streets.
I noted : colors, sizes, fabrics,
and most important, sites of find.
I stopped abruptly despite traffic
and wrote small in a small spiral book,
positive at that cold moment
that someone else could come to believe
this information made a poem.

CONVENIENCE

The pavement's cracked to accommodate
straining roots of sycamores
inconveniently lining narrow streets,
forcing young mothers, hired nannies,
to maneuver strollers
to reach the neighborhood park.

Now someone ought to *do something*—
level that pavement,
chop down those ugly tree roots,
make the sidewalk safe
for toddlers on their scooters.
So maybe some trees don't survive.

BUILDING SITES—SUNDAY

1.
A Graham dancer,
the construction crane
angles motionless
against the pale sky.

2.
Backhoe is kneeling,
neck bent wearily.
Precious day of rest.

STORIES

We grow up with metaphors we know nothing about. Take Jack and the beanstalk. I was a child in sandy Coney Island—what could I know about beanstalks? Take Hansel and Gretel wandering the dark forest. I lived yards from the ocean—how could I know about forests? The only trees around were sidewalk pets. Take goats crossing bridges. We had a box turtle in a backyard. I'd wave it around to scare other girls. It paddled its lizardly legs and craned its neck at this new means of locomotion. There were stray cats and family dogs and one boy owned a pony but he was rich. Alas, no geese with golden eggs were seen but once I got to watch puppies nurse—all eight of them—in a large cardboard box on our back porch.

WATER WORLD

A green drowning,
a breathing-in with no death at the end,
a pier's dark water,
winged seaweed
clinging to tar-coated pilings,
and a small child stunned
by a sun circling proudly
in unreachable blue.

VISITING MY CONEY ISLAND HOME

Carmela used to fuck for money
under this boardwalk.
Here's the stoop
where Francine's boyfriend shot her;
when we heard the news
we bathed the girls' room
of the Lincoln High School bathroom
with our tears.

Our mothers leaned calloused elbows
on window ledges of houses
that once crowded these empty lots
where crazy ladies are sifting for coins.
On his rare days off,
my roller-coaster hero father
would hold my hand
navigating Steeplechase Park;
it's this parking lot with the parachute jump
as lawn ornament.

They think the Mob
pushed the Jewish guy out the window
of the Half Moon Hotel back in the Forties.
When things got bad at home, my mother's sister
would check in there and swig whiskey
while my cousins roamed the hallways
waiting for my mother to take them
for skeeball and custard. I came along
to be part of the day.
Now the Half Moon's a nursing home,
filled with odors of incontinence.

Not everything has changed.
The Stillwell Avenue subway station
holds its old aromas
of piss and cotton candy.
Beyond the beach sand
sun-flung diamonds glitter the waves.
And mornings when elsewhere
the city revels in sun
fog still whitens the ocean-facing windows
and the old men still tell the weather
by the bell buoy's toll.

FALL MADNESS

I'm seventeen, huddled
with an outlaw boyfriend
on the porch of an empty house.
Our cigarettes spark and we kiss,
but the cold keeps me safe
from further exploration.
My books lie propped on the stairs.

I'm rushing home clutching books
through windy October streets,
dangerous lad abandoned
to his unscholarly ways.
I'm warm with thoughts of dinner and sex,
an A-student with a penchant for bad boys,
a would-be writer glowing and pale
beneath a Hunter's Moon.

HYPOTHETICAL DREAM OF A FORMER LOVER

You dream me back: my phone number
not quite recalled or not enough change
or the cell phone's dead.

You forget if we're supposed to meet
at your place on Garfield or that bar on Prince
or the snow's too deep or the cab has stalled.

You dream my voice, my words too faint
in the din of the smoke and old beer in the bar.
You're just about to touch my hand,

I'm just about to stroke your cheek,
and then it's over with a finger-snap jolt.
Oh, but you're sad that I've vanished,

taking all those nights
and long blonde hair.

REMEMBRANCE OF THINGS

If I die first take an armful of my books—
paperbacks only—in a shopping bag,
take the subway to West Fourth Street,
and sell them to that guy with the folding table

who sets up every day outside the college library.
Take whatever dollars he decides they're worth
and get yourself a chocolate bar
and a cup of tea with the money.

Later a thin young woman will stop and scan that table
before beginning her evening's studies.
She'll riffle through the pages of one of those books,
its edges swollen by an unexpected rain.

She'll see my penciled marginalia,
shrug and pay her dollar
and slip the book into her faded tote bag,
next to an orange and her notes on Proust.

Two

EROTICA

Lie here
with me.
I'll teach you
something
if you let me
touch you
here
and here.
Lie here.
Let me.

AS A WOMAN MIGHT

Sometimes
after it rains in the city
the land lies flat and open
as a woman might,

when after sex
she presses her back, her legs
against the mattress,
her torso gleaming

like an avenue
that seems to shrug in the clear gray air,
stretching toward unseeable
high-ceilinged clouds.

LATE SEX

We play at eternal youth.
With care.
I am your body,
your body.
A little drunk.
No little feat.
All the tall buildings
across the river light up
with dusk joy.

BEGINNINGS

January 16:
After the first kiss
you vanish
down the moving stairs
into the deepest subway station.
Eurydice in command,
you do not turn back
to see me press my head
against the iron turnstile
with its odor of old keys,
cold as January.

February 16:
This afternoon
somewhere between
the Spanish bakery
and the Arab grocery
the pain abated
and with it my belief
that whenever you leave me
you're gone.
I kept walking,
even bought one pear,
a yam and some salad,
as if food mattered,
when what mattered
reached to us both on the blue air
like the webbing of a thin silk scarf.

March 16:
Rehearsing an ending I tease my tongue
with some infraction you've committed
and say I need to leave.
It excites me to hurt you in fantasy.
Then I remember
how we first entered my bedroom
trailing our black clothes.

April 16:
A gleaming silver hair
lies curled on my parquet floor.
I pick it up,
pull it through closed teeth
with my fingers,
wet it between my lips
as one preps thread
for needle,
not once but over and over,
soothing myself with this strand
that I could bite and break
just like that.

BROWNSTONE

I want to draw this room:
amber-colored bookcase, milk-pale fireplace;
print over the mantel of the nude
lying in flowers that echo the deep green carpet;
the two hefty Dantes—one gilt, one polychrome—
bookends baring stern faces to the afternoon sun;
how the new leaves of the local tree
stipple their shadows over the white wall
where the stereo sits on the glass shelf.

I want to draw the black and white cat
that sleeps on the black leather chair,
and the striped one that dozes on the couch;
how the huge amaryllis on the windowsill,
redder than the reddening sun,
commands attention;
the dust on the air;
the box of logs ready for next winter
(artificial logs, swaddled in red wrappers).

I want to draw the scent of cinnamon
you sprinkled in the coffee;
my trembling when you touched my face;
the tiny clatter of the cat dish in the kitchen;
the cold white wine's green taste;
your heartbeat;
the coo of pigeons under the air conditioner;
Bach.

SUNDAY MORNING, EARLY SUMMER

Old pollen and bird shit had glazed the window,
made milky the visible strip of sky,
softened the plane tree's branches,
left them waving in non-existent fog.

We could have cleaned the mess with a rag and soap,
or, even better, ammonia and paper,
turned pigeon shadows back into solid birds,
and unblurred the thick green ivy
that covered the wall in the neighbor's garden.

Instead, we stayed in bed,
listened to unnamed songbirds,
church bells and wind chimes,
and discussed rational actions,
their consequences,
and the role of blind luck.

A SORT OF EPITHALAMION

Whenever we pass
your old place on Clinton
I try to look into the window,
to see if the kitchen's been painted
and the fridge replaced.

But who could forget
the always unmade bed,
the mosquitoes that invaded the A/C sleeve,
how you flooded Barry's apartment
in your unique attempt to defrost the fridge.

Wine glasses crowding the sink,
the scratchy loveseat that you loved,
the years commuting
from my place to yours,
pushing the outside bell to enter excitement

as you ran down the stairs to let me in.
Wine, olives and over-aged cheese, and once
nothing but a can of tuna no mayo
for a late-night meal.
Great morning coffee.

Now my place is ours
and we buy tables, wallpaper and kitchen shelves.
Bed-making, after lovemaking, fridge full
of fruit, nuts, and cheese
that never has time to mold.

VERY EARLY ONE MORNING

Your heart beats under bones,
thuds in my ear, pressed there.
I slide my hand
over a nest of hair
nestling there. Ribs.
I run my fingers through. Thud.
Steady. Snore gently.
Don't wake yet. Pulse
beneath my hand. Please.

URBAN BIRD LIFE

Curiosity Crow's feathers
faintgleam in thin sun.
Urban bird,
hip to the danger of branches
dripping brown tendrils
of audiotape,
he won't be grabbed
by plastic bag.
He'll sharpbill
his way to safety
if need be.

BROOKLYN HEIGHTS, SEPTEMBER 12, 2001

You started crying
in Tony's restaurant,
your old firehouse
around the corner,
ashes and deaths
across the river.

I picture you years before—
young, uniformed,
commanding and comforting.
Now I'm trying to comfort you.
Who cares, who cares
if everyone sees you crying?

MOMENT OF SILENCE: THE SECOND YEAR

"TO OUR FALLEN BROTHERS—
YOU WILL NEVER BE FORGOTTEN
CHIEF MAHNKEN
BATTALION 38"

is written in black marker
by your daughter
across the front of your fireman red shirt
and hung, among other offerings,
on the Brooklyn Promenade fence,
while at the Transit Authority construction site below
an even dozen guys in hard hats
form a circle and bow their heads,

and when they scatter moments later
several of them make the sign of the cross,
while further down the Promenade
a Jewish congregation is gathered,
blowing the *shofar* through the crowd,
and over at the entrance
a local tenor sings "God Bless America."

Now the guys are back to straddling beams,
the Jews to praying.
Neighbors and tourists disperse quietly,
heading for coffee.
Before the day's end
someone will grab your shirt for a keepsake.
People do things like that.

HOW TO LOWER YOUR ANXIETY AFTER 9/11

Observe the bunker under construction
   across the street.
It will shelter officials in the event of
   another attack.
Observe the absence across the river.
   Now turn
from the window and focus on
   your stuff:
books, music, vases and rugs. They will
   keep you calm.

IN THE SICILY-ROME AMERICAN CEMETERY NOVEMBER 2001

Eight thousand headstones,
"arranged in gentle arcs," (quote, courtesy
American Battle Monuments Commission)—
a year's worth of killing.
Two flags slap softly in the wind,
flat-topped Roman pines stand guard,
a last polyantha rose carries its burden of fragrance,
and all the butterflies are white.

Further North, in ancient hill towns of Tuscany,
people believed they were forever protected by height.
Now we view the TV footage of the death
of a vertical city of steel and glass,
the ashes of fire chiefs, brokers, busboys, girls in boots,
and learn that history ceaselessly teaches us otherwise.

PATRIOT RANT

Stand by your Man
your flag
your waves of grain.
Maintain
those mountain majesties
and wave away
that momentary pang.
We're climbing
Jacob's Ladder as it leans
against the Appalachians.
Stand by your coal mine
nuclear stockpile.
Let the oil flow
and the banner wave.
Support our orange stands
as helpless ancient olive groves
go down.
We fly through spacious skies
to Vegas not Havana.
I'm tired and poor, Lady.
Can you help me out?

IF YOU KNEW THEN...

I.
Hitler sits across
the table. He holds
a weapon. I hold
a weapon. I have
never fired it.
Hitler smiles. He says,
"Kill me this second
or I will kill a
million or so Jews
within the next few
days." I say, "How do
I know you'll keep your
word?" So Hitler says,
"Trust me." So I trust
him. So I fire my
weapon. Nothing happens.

II.
Hitler sits across
the table, blah, blah,
blah. So I say, "Why
don't you not kill them?"
So he says, "O.K."
I don't trust him. So
I fire my weapon.
Nothing happens.

III.
Hitler sits blah, blah,
blah. So he says, "I'll
think about it." So
I trust him and I
don't fire my weapon.
Nothing happens.

IV.
Hitler blah, blah, blah.
So I fire and he
fires and the next day
a million Jews...

Three

WEST FOURTH STREET STATION

Five years dead now   how can I be passing you on a subway station   what are you doing on this subway station this late at night   where's your lover where's your taxi   bitch   five years dead   don't turn up here now on this subway station   she has your stooped shoulders   bun of black hair   black coat   black slacks   black shoes   the right height

If I pass her you'll be there   how can you be there   why don't you answer when I call your name   I won't call your name   you died five years ago   this is no dream   this is no dream   you can be here and you can be dead   I'll call your name   this stooped woman can't answer to your name   you can't answer to your name   you're dead bitch   what are you doing here

TWO FOR WILLIAM PACKARD

ELEGY FOR BILL

I didn't know him
until after the stroke
so I just don't know
what he could have been like
before he had to
bump down the stairs ass first
to reach the street, then
haul his ass back after
he made that short trip
to Seventh Avenue
to have his quick meal
at the Chelsea Diner
whenever he was
able to get someone
to wheel him over.
If not, what did he do
for food? I don't know.
Could being hungry and
being helpless turn
a poet so mean?

WHERE I AM WHEN I FIND OUT

I go with Philip to get his butt checked
by the doctor on the Upper East Side
and I step outside to use my cell phone
to return Raymond's urgent e-mail
thinking the screening's been cancelled.
Ray tells me Bill died while writing—
dropped the pen, went to sleep.

I say nothing to Philip,
just take out the crossword puzzle
to keep us busy while waiting.
I'm feeling nothing. I won't miss
that bizarre apartment or screening
those bad poems every month
or his kicking ass at NYU
in overcrowded classrooms.

Fuck! I'm starting to get angry.
Who's going to keep
those Latinate words
at bay? Goodbye, Bill.

MY DEAD MOTHER COMES TO MY IMAGINARY POETRY READING

No, please
don't sit
all the way
back there.
Yes, you
look fine.
No one
will notice
your teeth.
I know
you're nervous.
I can tell
by your
grim mouth.

You're wondering
why I insisted
you come.
I could have
described it
to you later
and given you
a copy
of the program
with my name
listed.
We could have
sat in
your kitchen

on the
aluminum chairs
drinking
your good coffee.
You would
not have asked me
to read
any poems to you.
But you're here.
I sent the taxi
to bring you to
this dark room
below the restaurant.
There's a bar
at the back.
I've brought you
some coffee
but it's stale
and there was no
cream.
Now listen.
I will read four poems.
Only one
may upset you.
It's about
me.
The others are
about trees and other people.

You won't
relax your hold
on the cup
until
I finish reading and
everyone
applauds.
You'll say, "Very nice,"
with a tight smile
and begin
to move toward
the door.
If I were with
anyone but you

I'd ask,
"Want to have a drink?"
but I'll know how badly
you want to be home.
"Tell me …." I'll start to say
but I'll find you a cab instead.
You'll be home soon.
I'll have tipped the driver.
I'll be getting high
on white wine
with other poets.
You'll be riding that taxi.
I hope you're smiling.

THE DRINKING LIVES

Now Shirley's dead and Barry's fucked up with Alzheimer's but I think of a sweet time when we sat in the window of the gay bar on Bleecker and remembering the smell of that alcohol takes me further back to Larry's place on Prince Street where I burned my elbow in the open gas jet in the bathroom down the hall while I was kissing someone whose name I don't remember and I was so drunk I didn't feel a thing.

I have a new lover and we drink too much wine but I never drink Scotch anymore because of Rose which is strange because she drank martinis which smell nothing like Scotch but yet the smell of Scotch is the smell of Jerry's Restaurant on Lexington where Rose could hold her own with the Irish guys but this was before the Citicorp Building was erected and Jerry's was torn down.

My lover's out of town but those ghosts will hang around until he's back in Brooklyn with bottles of special wine that we'll take to restaurants with no corkage fee and we'll drink each other many toasts but when we get back to his place and he plays those Argentine love songs by Carlos Gardel and opens another bottle of wine I'll be toasting Rose.

DEAD ARTIST OPENING
for Bruce Rosen

We're matching
his paintings to his poems
trying to assign appropriate meanings
before everything is shipped to the gallery
while Bruce smiles amused
from wherever he is
or isn't:

"Girls, girls,
meaning is whatever the universe decides.
You will never figure it out.
But I thank you for trying."

HAUNTED

After you died I bought a bottle of your scent
from a turbaned hawker on the street,
and wore it awhile, a little defiant, a little nervous.
But it never suited my skin (too fair)
or my hair (too light), so I threw it away,
wanting to be wanted for the woman I am.

The night before you died,
you finally recovered consciousness
so the staff stopped asking
if you spoke any English,
you who were perfect in any language.

As I got up to leave, I steeled myself
and said, "I've never loved anyone like I've loved you."
You repeated the words back to me
and warned, "Be here when I wake up tomorrow,"
but I was a little too late.

ANTONY ABANDONS DIONYSUS
after Constantine Cavafy

How you left—
at midnight.
Your posse beat their drums,
creating the rhythm of leaving.
And then you were gone,
leaving me to pack, alone,
and wait for morning.
Dawn light
hid the fading drumbeats
already miles away,
and you constantly shuttling
from front to back of the line,
your dancing form all flashing lights.

Light grew
and I stumbled out of my house
and started down the street,
away from the way you'd gone.
By then,
tears dried, coffee drunk,
I'd swept dusty vine leaves
from the corners. But I left
the door ajar, preferring the danger
of thieves over darkness.

I'm a mile away now.
The City sounds are almost gone.
I'm approaching the sea, and the air
is freshening with salt.
I picture you
turning your party from their path
and tracing back the way to my house.
The breeze will have cleansed
the remaining vine leaves from the rooms.
Everyone will settle down,
strum instruments, tap rhythms.
You as well. And I'll be gone.

SHYLOCK, AFTER

A bitter baptism,
no gentle rain,
has soaked his shoulders.
He shudders as he ends his scene
and moves offstage,
swallowing history's bile.

EDWARD HOPPER IN NYACK

He's dreaming again
of the light of empty spaces,
shadows and sun,
corners of daylight.

It's always daylight in his dreams,
sun on walls, no one
inhaling the hot dust,
only floorboards striped by dazzle,
only corners dazed by lack of shade.

BARTLEBY AT REST

I inhabit the space at the back,
a wall my view—
bleached bricks and occasional flash of sun—
until I don't anymore,
yet leaving is unimaginable now.

I perch in the staircase.
Wrought iron railings and hollowed marble steps.
Everything is vertical, vertiginous.
He finds me there. He understands
everything unnecessary to me.

There is nothing he can say,
only to leave me alone.
Now these other iron bars clang
as if meant to keep sleep away.
I know other ways now.

RALPH EUGENE MEATYARD PHOTOGRAPHY EXHIBIT

Nothing ever happens
by chance in these photos.
You arrange your children
so their lives gleam against
old wallpaper, worn boards.
It's mostly fun to them,

posing with masks and dolls
to humor their daddy.
They know they're just posing.
Their grinning faces tell
us it's just another
way to spend a Sunday.

Maybe they'd rather be
doing unposed kid stuff,
whatever kids did back
in the fifties before
video games, maybe
football. When you've made them

sulk or stare we know it's
just for the camera. They're
not really so dour. They
like abandoned houses,
high grass. What kids wouldn't?

MY NEXT DUCHESS

That's my next duchess
wandering the kitchen garden
skirts swirling among the lettuces
gathering earth mold and insects
which she thinks, if she does,
she'll carry in with her when she
decides to stop her circling
and assume her proper role within.

My guest, I beg you pardon her.
She's yet to learn our ways.
She comes from a place where the rules
of rank are somewhat loose.
She has potential, and I'm assured
that I've allotted her sufficient time
to trim her awkwardness
as she trims her skirts of garden dirt.

I trust by your next visit
she'll stand with me,
greet you properly and walk
beside us up these stairs
to view my gallery. I know you'll find
much there, on walls and niches,
to ponder and admire.
She finds it chilling,

but she comes from a warmer
clime. She's settling down already,
I've observed. Her father, from
older, nobler family than even mine,
assures me of her virtues and that
she will be the perfect wife to grace
my table, home and bed. I'm patient.
Look—she comes toward us as we speak.

THE LAST OF THE DUKE

Devil, standing
on his marble terrace,
that fat sycophant beside him,
waiting, fingers drumming,
for me to trade
this sunlit garden
for this mausoleum of a "home."

Devil, really thinking
no one's told me that he's guilty,
and why that portrait's so important
that every guest
is made to stand
and mutter compliments
to its creator and its owner.

Devil, do you think
I'd let you know what's growing
in your so-well tended kitchen garden,
or that your gardener thinks of you as I do,
and so he's handed me
a bunch of yew seeds
which, if you took an interest

in anything besides your art and title,
you'd know will kill you quicker
than all assassins put together.
So stand there, hold your pose.
It won't take long. I'll join you.
I'll pour your brandy.
Sip it while her portrait smiles.

EN ATTENDANT BECKETT

Old Sam awaits the two of them. The tree's
in leaf. Or not. The moon is up. Or down.
He's been on center stage beside this mound
since yesterday and waits for his release.
Two tramps—though not in mud—have chained him to
the stage. He waits. How nice if all these hours
should lead to recognition of his power
to show with silent gesture and a few
choice words how beautiful and barren all
seems now. Yet he's post-modernly become
his own portrayer of the futile dumb
show where his conjured tramps should strut and crawl.
You've left yourself no exit, Sam, no way
to end this mad enigma of a play.

Four

"That time of year thou mayst in me behold..."

Much colder. Birds stir
the ivy. He leans
on the elm to catch
his breath. She gathers
firewood. He tightens
his scarf. Takes her arm.
Pushes himself off
the tree with effort.
She hands him a rake.
Shivers. A bat flits
across ink-blue sky.
They smile and head up
the dead-leafed path. Get
home in time for tea.

RAIN

Rain at the window:
the hissing misery of sleet.

I stare out—a membrane seems to give
and the weather enters the room.

The fragile barrier between
smug safety and wild air is gone.

CADMAN PLAZA PARK AT 8AM

Raingreen scent. I want to roll
like a pup until I'm soaked.
Until I turn raingreen. And shiver.
The rain's over, been over
for some hours. The park's become
a sunstruck raingreen
spot. Where god it sparkles.

CHILLY FOR MAY

There's a cold rain but a pale line in the west sky means the old rain will soon end and the dry wind in the wet sky bring a cool moon and the wet oak soaked by cold rain will shed wet leaves so the full moon and the sharp stars in the cold sky will leave pale streaks on the wet leaves on the soaked ground in this cool month.

BELIEVE

Believe in the small god
who sweeps the blue wind forward
in late November,
scatters small mammals
around oak trunks,
turns the air outside our houses
crisp and bitter.
And believe that he can ice our dreams
so we wake shivering,
aware that he controls
something more than autumn.

GREEN SURVIVOR

Gingko flings archaic branches
asymmetrically
against the sky. Cousin to the giant fern,
survivor of dynasties,
it once nurtured dinosaurs
bent on devouring its fan-shaped leaves.
Through Earth's ages,
Gingko has survived
as swamps turned into forests
and spores into seeds.

It lives now in my city
and I bow
to its green longevity,
willing it to survive its current foes—
street-faced children
with their bikes and knives,
Asian women
grabbing for its smelly harvest—
willing it to keep waving those branches
wackily
while rooted solidly
in the tender shell of the turtle
that carries the weight of the world
on its back.

WALKING WITH LAURIN

Walking with Laurin through brown leaves:
she, in her second autumn,
crushing the crackling bounty of a single season
with her little blue shoes.
Her feet are new to the earth
but already she's gleefully claiming her human heritage,
her right to convert the stuff of nature
into child-size pieces.

LOW TIDE

Under sky whose breath
sets the bay lightly rocking
girl and grandfather wear
identical yellow t-shirts
that spell Cape Cod
in pink curled shrimps.
Her plastic flip-flops lie nearby,
nearly covered with sand.
They're searching for
shelled treasures.
She pokes a stick and shrieks
as a tiny crab is teased
from beneath a damp striped rock
and cries, "Did we kill it?
Instantly grandfather swings her
over his shoulders, turning her face
toward shore's edge
where the sandpipers peep and peep.

NIGHT STORM AT THE BEACH

Rain has soaked the window shades.
In the morning the towels
are still damp.

I wake before the children
next cottage down begin to
race about,

and remember the lightning,
how it bleached the walls of this
tiny house.

ATLANTIC—6:45 a.m.

An orange band ignites the air,
stripes the water, heals the scars
from diving birds and dolphins' fins.

I missed the dawn by minutes
but got to see a wet black Lab
hurl its bulky shape

enthusiastically toward Spain,
scattering sandpipers.
They shrieked like tiny teenage girls.

SOMETHING LIKE PEACE

The trickling fountain
with its bathing birds
becomes my mind.
Old myths, old tales
spill from tier to tier
while robins and jays fly in
and soon depart refreshed.
And I, too, am refreshed
and all my muscles are loose.

ARS POETICA

Poetry is that naughty child
who skips wildly down the street
but glances back
every so often
to reassure itself
that it won't be captured
easily
but that it will be captured
before it's totally
out of control.

BIRTH CRIES

"If the universe is created with a bang but no one is around to witness it, does it still make a sound?"
—The New York Times 6/8/04

Out of the ear of Universe
springs Athena
as Big Bang rings changes
on gods and time. A wise child
knows her Dad.

TEMPUS FUGIT

The old pilot Time
screams through the sky,
his beard too sparse to flow.
He resembles Ezra Pound but fiercer.
Too shrewd to risk a cold,
He keeps the cockpit closed.
A thinness of air
facilitates his speed.
Necks bent awkwardly,
we look up,
but he's gone.

UNTETHERED

In the '50's sci-fi film
the space traveler repairs
his spaceship's skin.
He kneels, his special boots
lose contact with his craft,
he floats away.

"Grab me, grab the tether!"
his fellow traveler cries
but he can't, he keeps floating away,
out of reach,
out there for good,
lost in space.

Now nothing but gentle tumbling;
unwilling unlucky new planet
circling no sun;
close your eyes it's just the same,
dust, dust, stardust.

Earth gone,
and firm ground
and time and even memory;
no ship no comrades
no body. Nobody
in his sight, by his side.

It's ending.
Spaceman remains
where he is, where he was,
turning, turning, free.

ACCUMULATIONS

We store old dreams just in case:
the magic flying ones,
the ones composed of beasts and fear,
of the dead and the pleasing.

If you doze, one of them,
a mythical visitor, may jump
the barrier your brain's erected
and crash the rhythm of your day.

PLAYGROUND SCIENCE

After a heavy rain the swings' wet wood
swells and softens. The children's fingers
press against the surface and they feel
the whorls and bumps that live
hidden during dry days.

The children can't wait. They fling
themselves on the seats and pump themselves up
into the new air. Later their shorts will be damp
and their butts cold. But who cares?
This suddenly sun-blue afternoon

belongs to them. Blur by blur
they learn the science of motion,
climbing the sky, higher, higher,
then earth-pull, swoop-back, feeling
shivers in their small bellies,

the shivers they'll feel again
when they're moving their bodies
through the grown-up paces of sex,
and they'll wonder why
that pull and swoop feel so familiar.

WHAT YOU LEARN IN THE DARK

On the Cape's Nauset Beach
one damp summer night
families follow Park Ranger
down the steep dune.
Fathers tote children on their shoulders;
mothers drag canvas bags filled
with special shells, sand-sprinkled sandwiches
and other beach-day debris.
We follow instructions and lie in a row.
The sand feels cold.
Nervous children grab for parents' hands.

The lesson for tonight—
an owl's ears are not symmetrical.
In the dune darkness, gritty dampness,
we all nod. Ranger says the owl
uses its asymmetrical ears
to target its prey in the exacting night
without help from the moon
or the Milky Way's dusty basket.
We, symmetrical-eared,
can't swoop with confidence,
can't know what the talon feels
as it sinks assuredly
into the flesh of rabbit or field mouse.

"Can you swivel your heads all the way around
the way the owl can, children?"
asks Ranger out of the darkness.
The children crane hopefully,
soft unfeathered cheeks
brushing the rough sand,
but they can't do what the owl can.

NOT SWAN LAKE

Pigeons pirouette above the park,
visible through November branches.
Sun spotlights their choreography,
their barely seen wings
transforming from dove gray
to paper white over and over.
A second smaller corps
veers directly toward the first,
joining, then turning, as one.

From my high window view I'm reminded
of the breath-holding moment at the ballet
when from the second balcony we worry
that the tutu-clad dancers will collide—
but they never do.

WHAT STIRS

The park in summer. August heat.
Haunched on the grass
a dark-furred squirrel chews on a gleaning.
It stares at me and suddenly I know
why we believe in fairy tales, in animals
who speak, who comfort and advise,
and warn us of danger.
The air grows grayer.
If rain begins it will be gentle.

A piece of sycamore bark brushes my arm.
Two white butterflies mate giddily.
The heavy sky stirs debris of earlier weathers,
through which a brown rat
peeps up at me with shining eyes,
hoping for rain or the Princess
who promised to free him.
"No rain, no luck."—
what the squirrel said.

INSPIRATION

Read a poem the other   Guy admits
he used to kill frogs with a baseball
bat   Just batted them like baseballs
when he was   I thought shit
if he can write a poem
about   then I can   About how Janacek's
Violin Sonata seduced me
last night right in the middle of
About how I started to smile
as soon as   About how that
violin bow became
And stroked   And the piano
pounded then purred   And how
my smile got   And
no frogs were killed

IMPLAUSIBLE

I want to be the girl who brings the bucket of water
to the farm hands on hot August days when the sky
stretches thin its milky blueness.

I want the farm hands to push back their caps,
rub their dusty hands up and down on the legs of their overalls
before shyly passing that bucket around

and gratefully drinking the water
I'd hauled up with aching arms
from the well in the yard

while white and red chickens fluttered around,
beaks open, hoping for a trickle from the dripping bucket.
I want the farmer's wife to be plump but not fat,

with a soft tummy and comfortable large breasts,
and curly short hair going nicely gray. I want her
to toss the chickens their feed

with a balletic gesture of her arms,
so that the pale grains cloud the air
before raining down on the warm brown earth of the yard.

I want the tractor to be silent in its shed,
the barn cat to curl at my feet and my life to be summer.
I know it won't. I can live with that.

About the Author

Iris Lee is a poet and editor living in Brooklyn. She runs a writing workshop for theater professionals at the Actors Fund, and studies the poetry-theater connection at HB Studio. She has a professional background in Human Services, with all appropriate credentials. Lee is both a native New Yorker and Quaker. Her poems have appeared in print and on-line journals, including *Subway Chronicles*, *Passager*, and *The New York Quarterly*.

About NYQ Books™

NYQ Books™ was established in 2009 as an imprint of The New York Quarterly Foundation, Inc. Its mission is to augment the *New York Quarterly* poetry magazine by providing an additional venue for poets already published in the magazine. A lifelong dream of NYQ's founding editor, William Packard, NYQ Books™ has been made possible by both growing foundation support and new technology that was not available during William Packard's lifetime. We are proud to present these books to you and hope that you will continue to support The New York Quarterly Foundation, Inc. and our poets and that you will enjoy these other titles from NYQ Books™:

Joanna Crispi	*Soldier in the Grass*
Ted Jonathan	*Bones and Jokes*
Amanda J. Bradley	*Hints and Allegations*
Ira Joe Fisher	*Songs from an Earlier Century*
Kevin Pilkington	*In the Eyes of a Dog*

Please visit our website for these and other titles:

www.nyqbooks.org